60

Amen!
Godfried Cardinal Danneels

Kim En Joong

ont apporté leur collaboration à cet ouvrage

Alberto Fabio Ambrosio
Helen Frank
Gerda Hauch
Roger Matthys
Sung Hyuk
Alejandro Pérez

ISBN: 978-1-925438-15-4 (paperback)
978-1-925438-16-1 (hardback)
978-1-925438-17-8 (epub)
978-1-925438-18-5 (pdf)

ATF
FRANCE
www.atffrance.com
ATF France est une empreinte de ATF (Australia) Ltd
PO Box 504
Hindmarsh, SA 5007
Australie
ABN 90 116 359 963
www.atfpress.com
nouveaux horizons

Graphic Design & Layout: Lydia Paton
Fonts: Garamond (12pt) Carlton Plain (22pt)

Amen!

Godfried Cardinal Danneels

Kim En Joong

ATF
FRANCE

Introduction

Amen, c'est le titre donné au recueil de soixante reproductions de tableaux du P. Kim En Joong comprenant soixante paroles qui, pour célébrer le soixantième anniversaire de l'ordination sacerdotale du Cardinal Gottfried Danneels, archevêque émérite de Malines-Bruxelles et ancien primat de Belgique, ont été écrites, inscrites, à même la toile.

« Grace à la chasuble que le Cardinal m'avait demandée il y a bien longtemps de peindre pour lui personnellement, ce symbole de la charité qu'est la chasuble nous a enveloppés » écrit le P. Kim En Joong. De fait, le Cardinal Danneels qui a toujours témoigné d'une grande sensibilité aux arts et aux artistes en commençant par les primitifs flamands jusqu'à l'art abstrait de Kim En Joong, a aussi pratiqué la pastorale apostolique par l'art. Nombre de ses *Lettres de carême* par exemple sont des poèmes ou des prières, plutôt que des discours, partagés avec son peuple ; la chasuble est signe du souci du peuple et intercession pour le peuple : devant Dieu pour tous.

Cette charité fut encore pour le P. Kim la joie d'un accompagnement spirituel, personnel, et d'une fraternité sacerdotale vécue : le P. Kim a toute sa vie accordé une place importante à ce type de cheminement intergénérationnel. Venu de Corée pour participer en occident à la quête spirituelle de l'art abstrait par laquelle il rencontre la foi chrétienne jusqu'à être ordonné prêtre dans l'Ordre des prêcheurs, son engagement dans l'art quand il était jeune dominicain ne se comprend pas sans les encouragements du métaphysicien dominicain fribourgeois Louis-Bertrand Geiger, ou le Père Jean de Menasce d'origine hongroise qui, complètement paralysé et aphasique à la suite d'un accident cérébral, lui dactylographia difficilement avec un seul doigt ce message à propos de sa double vocation de prêtre et de peintre : « Dieu ne reprend jamais les dons qu'il fait aux hommes ». Et le P. Kim poursuit encore son entretien avec le Père Albert Patfoort décédé à plus de cent ans. Toutefois, pour comprendre ces relations, il faut entrer dans une culture et une grammaire qui n'est pas occidentale --elle fait même parfois cruellement défaut, mais asiatique : le culte et la vénération des anciens.

Pour exprimer cette relation la tradition des calligraphes d'Asie était la mieux appropriée : ce n'est pas un artifice esthétique, factice ou mondain car cette relation s'inscrit dans la tradition asiatique. De plus, le Cardinal Danneels, inaugurant à la basilique de Brioude le plus grand chantier de vitraux du XXI° siècle en France, déclarait au moment de bénir les trente-six vitraux du P. Kim : « Aujourd'hui la vérité semble inaccessible et incertaine, le bien trop difficile et exigeant, mais la beauté désarme. » De fait le P. Kim a prêché par les pinceaux tout au long de sa vie et le Cardinal tout au long de sa vie sacerdotale exercé le ministère par une pastorale du stylo, la poésie, la prière. On s'en souvient, lorsque les tanks soviétiques écrasèrent le soulèvement de Budapest en 1956, la police politique vint perquisitionner l'appartement du philosophe György Lukacs et d'emblée lui intima l'ordre de remettre les armes en sa possession ; alors, le philosophe prit dans sa poche son stylo et le tendit.

Déjà le P. Kim avait offert au Cardinal un livre recueillant quatre-vingt céramiques pour célébrer l'exploit, comme dit le psalmiste, de ses quatre-vingts ans. Mais selon le calendrier lunaire dans la tradition asiatique soixante est un cycle parfait et le reste à venir est grâce et surcroit.

Amen, « en vérité~ainsi-soit'il », revient quatorze fois dans la Bible hébraïque. C'est pendant et après la période du second Temple que ce mot a pris une importance durable dans la liturgie synagogale comme réponse à la bénédiction des prêtres et aux prières. Les chrétiens (et dans une moindre mesure les musulmans) l'ont repris de l'office chanté des lévites, les prêtres.

Et selon la tradition rabbinique juive, pour échapper à toute damnation, il suffit aux pécheurs comme à tout homme juste, de dire « Amen », *une seule fois.*

Ainsi est offert le livre *Amen*, prière et bénédiction, à l'occasion des soixante ans de presbytérat du Cardinal Danneels, une œuvre de parole et d'art, une œuvre à quatre mains : les mains de l'artiste dans sa quête spirituelle, mystique et apophatique –la prédication muette de Fra Angelico -- et la prière personnelle et pastorale du prêtre.

Et nous-mêmes qui prenons en main ce livre, avec émotion et joie nous répondons « Amen. »

NICOLAS JEAN SÉD

Introduction

Amen is the title given to the collection of sixty reproductions of paintings by Father Kim En Joong, including sixty words which, in celebration of the sixtieth anniversary of the priestly ordination of Cardinal Gottfried Danneels, Archbishop Emeritus of Malines-Bruxelles and former Primate of Belgium, have been written, inscribed, next to the canvas.

'Thanks to the chasuble which the Cardinal had asked me to paint for him personally, this symbol of charity which is the chasuble has surrounded us', writes Father Kim En Joong. In fact, Cardinal Danneels, who has always shown great sensitivity to the arts and artists, starting with the Flemish primitives, to the abstract art of Kim En Joong, has also practised apostolic pastoral work through art. Many of his Letters of Lent, for example, are poems or prayers, rather than speeches, shared with his people; The chasuble is a sign of the concern for the people and intercession for the people: before God for all.

This charity was again for Father Kim the joy of a spiritual, personal accompaniment and of a lived priestly fraternity: Father Kim has always given an important place to this type of intergenerational journey. Coming from Korea to take part in the spiritual quest for abstract art in the West, through which he encountered the Christian faith until he was ordained a priest in the Order of Preachers, his involvement in art when he was a young Dominican isn't quite understandable without the encouragement of the Dominican metaphysician from Fribourg, Louis-Bertrand Geiger, or Father Jean de Menasce of Hungarian origin, who, completely paralysed and aphasic as a result of a brain injury, typed him with difficulty using a single finger this message about His double vocation as a priest and a painter: 'God never takes back the gifts he gives to men.' And Father Kim still continues his conversation with Father Albert Patfoort who died at an advanced age of over 100. However, in order to understand these relations, one must enter a culture and a grammar that is not Western–even sometimes cruelly flawed, but Asian: the worship and veneration of the ancients.

To express this relation, the tradition of the calligraphers of Asia was the most appropriate: it is not an aesthetic, artificial or worldly artifice, for this relation is part of the Asian tradition. Moreover, Cardinal Danneels, inaugurating at the Basilica of Brioude the largest building site of stained-glass windows of the 21st century in France, declared when blessing the thirty-six stained glass windows of Father Kim: 'Today the truth seems inaccessible and uncertain, far too difficult and demanding, but beauty disarms.' In fact Father Kim preached through the brushes throughout his life and the Cardinal throughout his life as a priest ministered through pen-ministry, poetry, prayer. When the Soviet tanks crushed the uprising in Budapest in 1956, the political police came to search the apartment of the philosopher György Lukacs and immediately ordered him to surrender the weapons in his possession. Then the philosopher took his pen from his pocket and held it out.

Already Father Kim has offered the Cardinal a book collecting eighty ceramics to celebrate the feat, as the psalmist says, of his eighty years. But according to the lunar calendar in the Asian tradition sixty is a perfect cycle and the rest to come is grace and extra.

Amen, 'in truth, so-be it', occurs fourteen times in the Hebrew Bible. It was during and after the Second Temple period that this word took on a lasting importance in the synagogal liturgy as a response to the blessing of priests and at prayers. The Christians (and to a lesser extent the Muslims) took it back from the chanted service of the Levites, the priests.

And according to Jewish rabbinical tradition, to escape all damnation, it is enough for sinners as for every righteous man, to say 'Amen', *only once*.

Thus the book *Amen*, Prayer and Blessing, is offered on the occasion of Cardinal Danneels' sixty years of presbyterate, a work of speech and art, a work with four hands: the hands of the artist in his spiritual quest, mystical and apophatic—the silent preaching of Fra Angelico—and the personal and pastoral prayer of the priest.

And we ourselves who take this book in hand, with emotion and joy, we reply, 'Amen'.

NICOLAS JEAN SÉD

Aphorism 1

Le rire colore toutes les journées même les plus sombres

Een glimlach kleurt de dagen, zelfs de donkerste

Laughter colors every day, even the darkest

Reír da color a todos los días incluso a los más oscuros

Ridere colora le giornate, soprattutto quelle più nere

Lachen gibt auch den düstersten Tagen Farbe

미소는 낮에는 물론 어두운 밤까지 환하게 한다

Le rire colore les pensé
même les plus sombres.

+ Godfried Car. Danneels

Aphorism 2

Toute bonne parole naît du silence

Goede woorden worden geboren in de stilte

Every good word is born from silence

Toda buena palabra nace del silencio

Ogni parola buona nasce dal silenzio

Jedes gute Wort wächst aus der Stille

유익한 말들은 침묵으로부터 나온다

Toute bonne parole
naît du silence

Aphorism 3

Le coeur gai guérit beaucoup de blessures

Een vrolijk hart geneest vele wonden

A happy heart heals many wounds

El corazón feliz cura muchas heridas

Il cuor leggero sana le ferite

Ein fröhlich' Herz heilt viele Wunden

밝은 마음은 쌓인 상처를 치유해준다

Aphorism 4

Pour être heureux il faut prendre le temps

Om gelukkig te zijn: neem tijd

To be happy takes time

Para ser feliz hay que tomar su tiempo

Per essere felici, occorre del tempo

Wer glücklich sein will, muss sich die Zeit dafür nehmen

행복하기 위해서는 시간이 필요하다

Pour être heureux, prends d'abord le temps!

+ Giuseppe Card. Bertone

Aphorism 5

Si tu dois aller loin, commence à faire le premier pas

Als je ver moet gaan, begin met de eerste stap

If you want to go a long way, start by taking the first step

Si debes ir lejos, comienza dando el primer paso

Se devi andare lontano, comincia a far il primo passo

Wenn Du einen weiten Weg vor Dir hast, beginne mit dem ersten Schritt

멀리 가기 위해서는 한 걸음부터 시작해야 한다

Si tu dois aller loin,
commence à faire
le premier pas

+ Godfried Card. Danneels

Aphorism 6

Le véritable amis est celui qui te dit ce que d'autres lui diront aprés ta mort

Hij die je nu al zegt wat anderen hem over jou na je dood zullen zeggen, is een ware vriend

The true friend is the one who tells you what others will say about you after your death

El verdadero amigo es aquél que te dice lo que otros dirán después de tu muerte

Il vero amico è chi ti dice ciò che altri gli diranno dopo la tua morte

Ein wahrer Freund sagt Dir heute, was andere ihm sagen nach Deinem Tod

진정한 친구는 당신 사후에 할 말을 지금 들려주는 사람이다

Le véritable ami
est celui qui te dit
ce d'autres lui diront
après ta mort

+ Godfried Card. Danneels

Aphorism 7

Le temps de Dieu: c'est maintenant

De tijd van God is 'nu'

The time of God is now

El tiempo de Dios, es ahora

Il tempo di Dio è adesso

Gottes Zeit ist das Jetzt

하느님의 시간은 바로 이 시각이다

Le temps de Dieu :
c'est maintenant

Aphorism 8

Sois et reste ce que tu es, on t'aimera

Wees en blijf jezelf, je zal bemind worden

Be and remain what you are: others will love you

Sé y no cambies, así te amarán

Fa di essere e di restare quel che sei: ti vorranno bene

Sei und bleibe, was Du bist: man wird Dich lieben

당신이 자연스러우면 사람들은 더 호감을 갖게 될 것이다

Sois et reste
ce que tu es:
on t'aimera

Aphorism 9

Sois patient; tout a son temps

Alles komt op zijn tijd, wees geduldig

Be patient; everything has its time

Sé paciente; todo a su tiempo

Sii paziente. Ogni cosa a suo tempo

Sei geduldig. Alles hat seine Zeit

인내하라. 세상사에는 다 때가 있다

Sois patient.
Tout a son temps

Aphorism 10

La force de Dieu: c'est la douceur

De kracht van God is zijn zachtheid

The strength of God is sweetness

La fuerza de Dios es su dulzura

La forza di Dio: è la dolcezza

Gottes Kraft : seine Sanftheit

하느님의 힘은 온화함이다

La force de Dieu :
c'est la douceur

Aphorism II

La plus belle musique est parfois le silence

Stilte is soms de mooiste muziek

The most beautiful music is sometimes silence

La más bella música es algunas veces el silencio

La musica più bella è talvolta il silenzio

Manchmal ist Stille die schönste Musik

가장 아름다운 음악은 때로는 침묵이다

La plus belle musique
est parfois le silence

Aphorism 12

C'est maintenant qu'il faut vivre

Het is nú dat we moeten leven

Now is the time for living

Es ahora cuando hay que vivir

E' adessc che bisogna vivere

Lebe hier und jetzt

살아야 하는 시간은 바로 이 시점이다

Pourquoi se presser ?
C'est maintenant qu'il faut
vivre

+ Georges [illegible]

Aphorism 13

Toute parole qui apaise est le fruit de l'arbre de vie

Elk woord dat rust brengt is vrucht van levensboom

Every word that calms is the fruit of the tree of life

Toda palabra que calma es el fruto del árbol de vida

Ogni parola pacificante è il frutto dell'albero della vita

Jedes Wort des Friedens kommt vom Baum des Lebens

마음을 달래주는 언어들은 생명의 나무에서 나오는 열매다

Toute parole qui apaise
est le fruit de l'arbre de

Aphorism 14

A côté d'un ami, la route sera moins longue

Naas teen vriend is de weg altijd minder lang

Having a friend by your side, the route will be shorter

Al lado de un amigo, el camino será menos largo

Accanto ad un amico, la strada sarà meno lunga

Mit einem Freund an der Seite ist der Weg weniger lang

친구가 곁에 있으면 갈 길이 그리 멀게 느껴지지 않는다

A côté d'un ami,
la route sera moins longue

Les paroles méchantes blessent comme le fil de l'épée

Kwetsende woorden kunnen snijden als een zwaard

Harsh words hurt like the edge of a sword

Las palabras malas hieren como el filo de la espada

Le parole cattive feriscono come lama di spada

Böse Worte verletzen wie Schwerthiebe

친절하지 않은 말은 칼날처럼 상처를 입힌다

Les paroles méchantes blessent
comme le fil de l'épée

Le juste devient toujours un Agneau, debout et transpercé

De rechtvaardige is altijd eem Lam dat rechtop wordt doorboord

The righteous person is always like a lamb, upright and pierced

El justo se convierte siempre en un Cordero, de pie y traspasado

Il giusto si fa sempre Agnello, in piedi e trafitto

Der Gerechte wird immer zum Lamm, aufrecht, durchbohrt

정의로운 사람은 언제나 가슴이 뚫려 서 있는 한 마리 양이다

Le juste devient toujours
un Agneau
debout et transpercé
+ Georges Card.

Aphorism 17

Tout début est difficile, toute fin encore plus

Elk begin is moeilijk; elk einde is nog moeilijker

All beginnings are difficult, every ending is even harder

Todo comienzo es difícil, todo fin lo es aún más

Ogni inizio è difficile, ogni fine ancor più

Aller Anfang ist schwer, jedes Ende schwerer

처음부터 일을 어렵게 느낀다면 나중에는 더 힘들 것이다

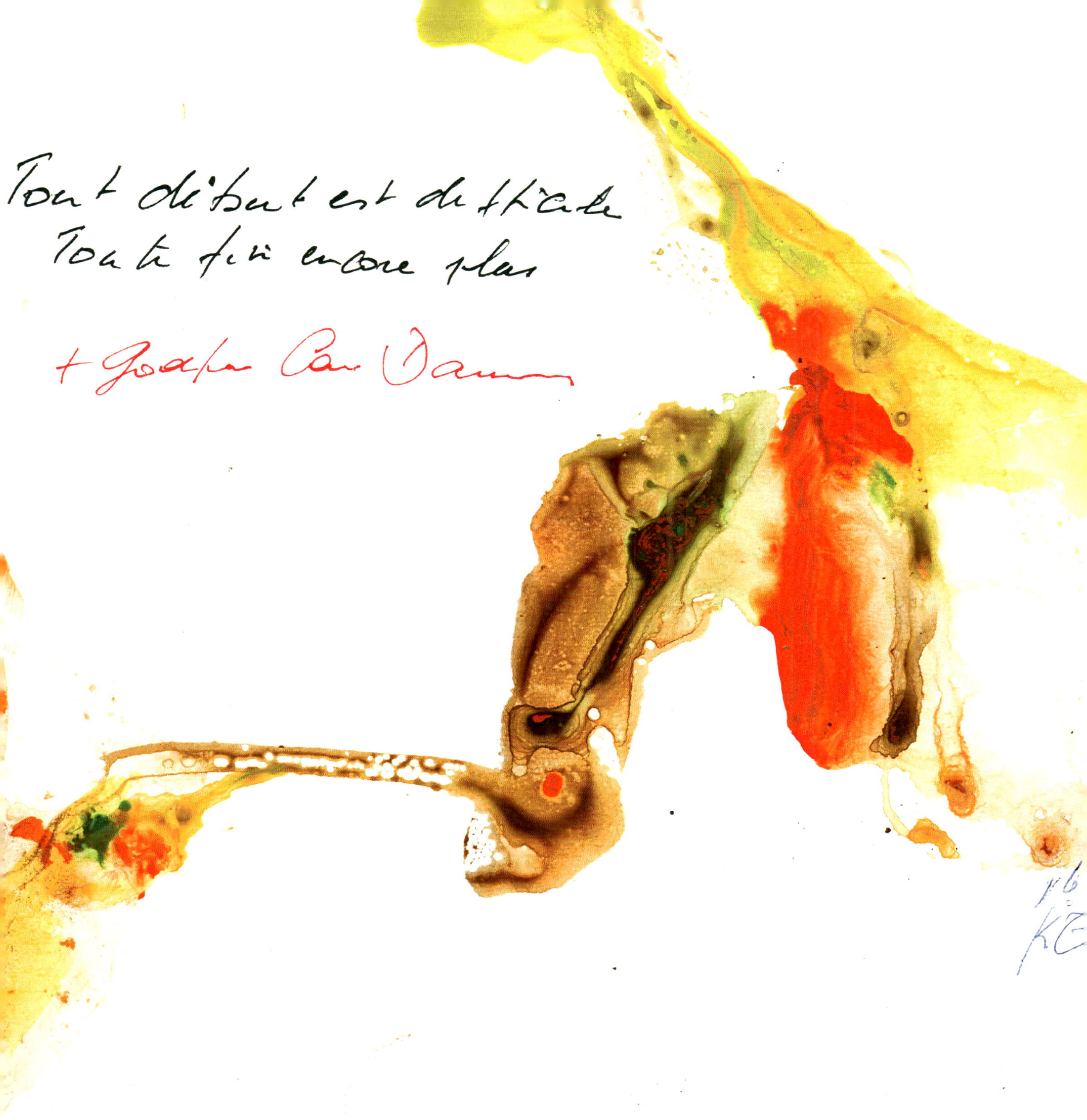
Tout début est difficile
Toute fin encore plus

Le juste est comme l'arbre de vie

De rechtvaardige is als een boom des levens

The righteous person is like the tree of life

El justo es como el árbol de la vida

Il giusto è come l'albero della vita

Der Gerechte ist wie der Baum des Lebens

정의는 생명의 나무와 같은 것이다

Le juste est comme l'arbre de vie

Aphorism 19

Pour bien entendre: apprends à écouter

Om goed te horen: leer luisteren

To hear well, learn to listen

Para entender bien: aprende a escuchar

Per sentire bene, impara ad ascoltare

Willst Du gut verstehen, lerne hören

이해를 잘 하기 위해서는 듣는 훈련부터 해야 한다

Pour bien entendre
apprends à écouter.

Aphorism 20

Qui se connaît soi-même ne juge pas les autres

Wie zichzelf kent, oordeelt niet over anderen

Those who know themselves do not judge others

Chi conosce se stesso non giudica gli altri

Quien se conoce a sí mismo no juzga a los demás

Wer sich selbst kennt, urteilt nicht über andere

자신을 잘 아는 사람은 다른 사람을 판단하지 않는다

Qui se connaît soi-même
ne juge pas les autres

Aphorism 21

Tous le rêves sont impossibles sauf le mien

Alle dromen zijn onmogelijk, behalve de mijne

All dreams are impossible except our own

Todos los sueños son imposibles salvo el mío

Tutti i sogni sono impossibili, salvo il mio

Alle Träume sind unmöglich, meiner nicht

내 꿈이 아니고는 다른 꿈들은 모두 허사다

Tous les rêves sont impossibles
sauf le mien

Dieu est simple (saint Jean Chrysostome)

God is eennvoudig (Sint Jan Chrysostomus)

God is simple (Saint John Chrysostom)

Dios es simple (San Juan Crisóstomo)

Dio è semplice (San Giovanni Crisostomo)

Gott ist einfach (Johannes Chrysostomus)

<하느님은 단순하시다> (요한 크리소스톰 성인)

"Dieu est simple."
(S. Jean Chrysostome)

Aphorism 23

Rien ne vielillit un homme comme un préjugé

Niets veroudert een mens zo sterk als een vooroordeel

Nothing ages one as much as prejudice

Nada envejece más a un hombre que los prejuicios

Nulla invecchia tanto quanto un uomo pregiudicato

Nichts lässt einen Menschen so altern wie ein Vorurteil

선입견처럼 사람을 늙게 하는 것은 없다

Rien ne vieillit un homme
comme un préjugé

Rorate coeli desuper et nubes pluant justum

Rorate coeli desuper et nubes pluant justum

Shower, O heavens, from above, and let the skies rain down righteousness

Ducha, oh cielos, desde arriba, y deja que el cielo llueva justicia

Stillate rugiada dall'altc, o cieli, e le nubi piovano il giusto

Tauet, Himmel, von oben! Wolken, regnet den Gerechten

하늘아, 높은 곳에서 정의를 이슬처럼 내려라. 구름아, 승리를 빗처럼 뿌려라

"Rorate coeli desuper
et nubes pluant justum
2016

Je demande à Dieu de me rendre moins compliqué

Mijn vragg aan God: me minder ingewikkeld te maken

I ask God to make me less complicated

Pido a Dios convertirme en alguien menos complicado

Chiedo a Dio di rendermi meno complicato

Lieber Gott, lass m ch weniger kompliziert sein

나 자신이 단순해지기를 하느님께 간구한다

Je demande à Dieu
de me rendre moins
compliqué

Aphorism 26

Dieu est le seul qui nous fait peur

God maakt niet bang maar Hij geeft vrees

God is the only one who can frighten us

Dios es el único a quien debemos temer

Dio è il solo a farci paura

Gott ist der einzige, der uns Angst machen kann

우리를 두렵게 하는 분은 오로지 하느님이시다

Dieu est le seul
qui nous fait peur

Ce qu'il y a le plus beau sur terre: la beauté du cie et le visage humain

Het mooiste op aarde: de schoonheid van de hemel en van het menselijk gelaat

The most beautiful thing on earth is the beauty of the sky and the human face

Lo más bello en el mundo: la belleza del cielo y el rostro humano

Quanto di più bello in terra: la bellezza del cielo ed il viso umano

Das Schönste auf Erden: die Schönheit des Himmels und die Gesichter der Menschen

지상에서 가장 아름다운 것은 창공의 아름다움과 사람의 얼굴이다

Ce qu'il y a de plus beau
sur terre:
la beauté du ciel
et le visage humain

Celui qui est conscient de prier, ne prie pas (Jean Cassien)

Hij die bewust meent te bidden, bidt niet (Jean Cassien)

One who is conscious of praying is not praying (John Cassian)

Aquél que es consciente de rezar, no reza (Juan Casiano)

Chi è cosciente di pregare, non sta pregando (Giovanni Cassiano)

Wer sich bewusst ist zu beten, betet nicht (Johannes Chrysostomus)

기도를 아는 사람은 자신이 기도한다는 사실을 의식하지 않는다 (요한 카센)

"Celui qui est conscient
de prier
ne prie pas."
(Jean Cassien)

Aphorism 29

Qui pose les vraies questions? l'enfant

Een kind stelt de ware vragen

Who pose the real questions? Children

¿Quién hace las verdaderas preguntas? Los niños

Chi fa le domande vere? Il bambino

Wer stellt die wahren Fragen? Das Kind

누가 진정한 질문을 던질 수 있는가? 바로 어린이다

Qui pose les vraies questions ?
L'enfant

Aphorism 30

Dieu nous prend comme nous sommes

God neemt ons zoals we zijn

God takes us as we are

Dios nos acepta como somos

Dio ci prende così come siamo

Gott nimmt uns, wie wir sind

하느님은 우리를 있는 그대로 받아들이신다

Dieu nous prend
comme nous sommes

La barque de Pierre a toujours balloté. Malheur à ceux qui ont mal de mer

Het bootje van Petrus heeft altijd gewankeld; spijtig voor hen die zeeziek worden

Peter's boat has always swayed. Woe to those who have sea sickness

El barco de Pedro siempre ha estado sacudido. Desgracia para aquellos que se marean

La barca di Pietro è sempre sballottata. Sfortuna per quanti hanno mal di mare

Petrus' Schiff schwankte und schwankt immer. Pech für die Seekranken

베드로의 배가 잠시도 파도에 편할 때가 없으니 멀미를 하는 사람은 불행하다

La barque de Pierre
a toujours ballotée.
Malheur à ceux
qui ont le mal de mer

+ Godfried Card. Danneels

Aphorism 32

Dire 'bonjour' donne de l'espérance

'Goeie dag' zeggen geeft hoop

Saying 'good-day' always gives hope

Decir 'buenos días' da la esperanza

Dire 'buongiorno' offre un po' di speranza

'Guten Tag' sagen schenkt Hoffnung

<인사>를 하는 것은 희망을 건네는 일이다

Dire 'bonjour' donne de l'espérance
+ Godfried Card. Danneels

Aphorism 33

La plus grande gloire: c'est l'humilité

Geen grotere eer dan de eenvoud

The greatest glory is humility

La más grande gloria: la humildad

La più grande gloria: è l'umiltà

Die grösste Ehre : die Demut

가장 영광스러운 것은 겸손이다

La plus grande gloire
c'est l'humilité

La puissance de Dieu: c'est la faiblesse

Zwakheid is Gods kracht

The power of God is weakness

La fuerza de Dios: su debilidad

La potenza di Dio: è la debolezza

Gottes Kraft: die Schwachheit

하느님의 강력한 힘은 약자에게 약하게 대하시는 것이다

La puissance de Dieu :
c'est la faiblesse

+ Godfried Card. Danneels

Aphorism 35

Toute loi appelle sa miséricorde

Elke wet roept op zijn barmhartigheid

Every law calls its own mercy

Toda ley pide su Misericordia

Ogni legge richiama la sua Misericordia

Jedes Gesetz verlangt auch Barmherzigkeit

법은 관용을 불러온다

Toute loi appelle
sa miséricorde

Aphorism 36

Le plus grand énigme c'est moi-même

Ikzelf ben het grootste raadsel

The biggest enigma is myself

El más grande enigma es uno mismo

Il più grande enigma son proprio io stesso

Das grösste Rätsel bin ich mir selbst

가장 큰 수수께끼는 나 자신이다

Le plus grand énigme
c'est moi-même

+ [illegible]

Aphorism 37

La pouvoir de Dieu: c'est la souffrance

Gods macht is zijn lijden

The power of God is suffering

La fuerza de Dios: el sufrimiento

Il potere di Dio: è la sofferenza

Gottes Macht : das Leiden

하느님의 위력은 고통이다

Le pouvoir de Dieu :
c'est la souffrance

Aphorism 38

Le trône de Dieu est le bois d'une croix

Gods troon is het kruishout

The throne of God is the wood of a cross

El trono de Dios es la madera de una cruz

Il trono di Dio: è il legno della croce

Gottes Thron : das Holz des Kreuzes

하느님의 왕위는 나무 십자가에 있다

Le trône de Dieu :
c'est le bois de la croix

Aphorism 39

Le nom de Dieu: c'est miséricorde

Gods naem is bramharttigheid

The name of God is mercy

El nombre de Dios: misericordia

Il nome di Dio: è la misericordia

Gottes Name: Barmherzigkeit

하느님의 이름은 자비다

Le nom de Dieu :
c'est la miséricorde

Aphorism 40

Dieu me demande peu. Il ne fait que tout donner

God vraagt me weinig; Hij geeft me alles

God asks little of me. He only gives everything

Dios me pide poco. Él se limita a dar todo

Dio poco mi chiede. Non fa che donare tutto

Gott fordert wenig von mir, geben tut er alles

하느님은 내게 아주 적게 요구하시지만 당신은 모두 다 주신다

Dieu ne demande rien
Il ne fait que tout donner

Aphorism 41

A l'homme de faire les projets; à Dieu la realisation

De mens wikt, maar God beschikt

Human beings make projects; God realises them

Es el hombre quien hace los proyectos; Dios quien los realiza

Sta all'uomo far progetti, a Dio realizzarli

Der Mensch macht Pläne, Gott setzt sie um

계획은 사람이 하고 그 실현은 하느님이 하신다

A l'homme de faire des projets
à Dieu la réalisation

+ Godfried Card. Danneels

Aphorism 42

Celui que se moque du pouvoir en veut beaucoup

Wie lacht met het gezag wil zelf machtig zijn

The one who laughs with authority wants to be powerful

El que se burla del poder lo desea mucho

Chi si burla del potere ne ricerca molto

Wer über Macht sich lustig macht, hätte gerne mehr

남의 권력을 하찮게 여기는 사람은 자신이 그것을 더 갖지 못해
조바심한다

Celui qui se moque du pouvoir en veut beaucoup.

+ [illegible]

Aphorism 43

Dieu a créé les hommes pour ne plus mourir

Om nooit meer te sterven schiep God de mens

God created human beings in order to die no more

Dios ha creado los hombres para que no mueran

Dio ha creato gli uomini per non più morire

Gott hat die Menschen geschaffen, um ewig zu leben

하느님은 사람이 더 이상 죽지 않도록 창조하셨다

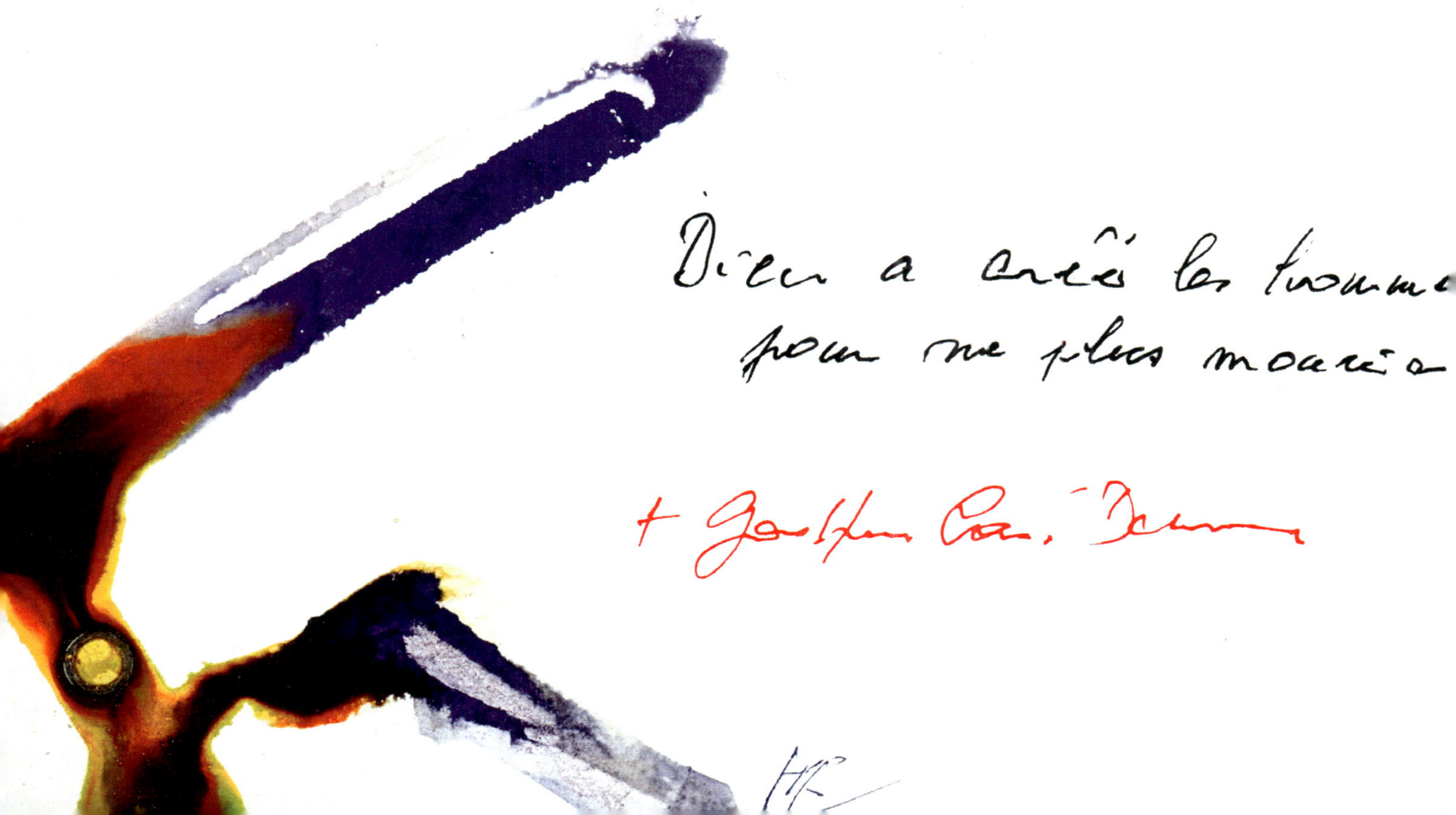
Dieu a créé les hommes
pour ne plus mourir

Aphorism 44

L'Espérance c'est la même chose que la gratuité, mais elle n'est pas l'utopie

Hoop is geen utopie

Hope is the same thing as freedom, but is not utopia

La speranza è la stessa cosa della gratuità, ma non è l'utopia.

La speranza non è utopia

Hoffnung und alles ist kostenlos sind dasselbe, aber Hoffnung ist keine Utopie.

희망은 무상과 같지만, 이상은 아니다

L'espérance, c'est la même chose
Que la gratuité,
mais elle n'est pas l'utopie

Aphorism 45

C'est la pluie qui vous fait apprécier le soleil

Regen doet ons naar de zon verlangen

It is the rain that makes you enjoy the sun

Es la lluvia que nos permite apreciar el sol

E' la pioggia che ci fa apprezzare il sole

Es ist wegen des Regens, dass wir die Sonne so schätzen

인간에게 가장 직접적으로 와 닿는 것은 태양이다

C'est la pluie
Qui nous fait apprécier
le soleil

+ [illegible]

Aphorism 46

Si tu dois aller lion, commence à faire le premier pas

Als je een lange weg wil gaan, zet de eerste stap

If you want to go a long way, start by taking the first step

Si debes ir lejos, comienza dando el primer paso

Se devi andare lontano, comincia a far il primo passo

Wenn Du einen weiten Weg vor Dir hast, beginne mit dem ersten Schritt

멀리 가려면 한 걸음부터 시작해야 한다

Als je een lange weg
wil gaan,
zet de eerste sta

A l'hoome les projets, à Dieu la décision

De mens wikt maar God beschikt

People put forward projects and God decides

Al hombre los proyectos, a Dios la decision

All'uomo competono i progetti, a Dio la realizzazione

Der Mensch macht Pläne, Gott verfügt darüber

계획은 사람이 하고 그 실현은 하느님이 하신다

De mens wikt
Maar God beschikt

Aphorism 48

Regarde avec ton coeur et ta vue est plus nette

Kijk met je hart, je ziet scherper

Look with your heart and your view is sharper

Mira con tu corazón y verás más claro

Guarda con il cucre per veder più chiaramente

Schau mit dem Herzen, dann siehst Du besser

마음으로 보게 되면 더 밝게 보인다

Kijk met het hart.
Je ziet scherper.

Aphorism 49

Pour bien entendre: écoutez!

Om goed te horen: luister!

To hear well, listen!

Para entender mejor, escucha!

Per sentire bene: ascolta!

Um gut zu hören - höre zu!

이해를 잘 하려면 잘 들어라

Om goed te horen: luister!

Aphorism 50

Qui occupe une haute place durable est souvent humble

Wie hoog staat op de maatschappelijke ladder is vaak een man die nederig is

Those who hold a solid high place on the social ladder are often the most humble

Quien ocupa un alto cargo es a menudo humilde

Chi occupa stabilmente un'alta carica spesso è umile

Wer auf der sozialen Leiter hoch oben steht, ist nicht selten demütig

높은 자리를 오랫동안 유지하는 사람은 보통 겸손하다

Wie hoog staat op de
maatschappelijke ladder
is vaak een man die nederig is

+ [illegible]

Aphorism 51

Le bonheur est une fleur; il faut la cultiver

Geluk is als een bloem, je moet ze verzorgen

Happiness is like a flower; you need to take care of it

La felicidad es como una flor: se debe cultivar

La felicità è un fiore. Bisogna coltivarlo

Das Glück ist eine Blume, die gepflegt sein will

행복은 꽃과 같아서 잘 가꾸어야만 한다

Geluk is als een bloem
je moet ze ook
verzorgen

Aphorism 52

Tout a son temps, soyez patient

Alles heft zijn tijd, daarom wees geduldig

Everything has its time, so be patient

Todo en su momento, sé paciente

Ogni cosa ha il proprio tempo. Abbiate pazienza

Alles zu seiner Zeit: nur Geduld

세상만사에는 때가 있으니 인내심을 가져야 한다

Alles heeft zijn tijd:
Daarom wees

Le nom de Dieu: c'est miséricorde

Gods naam is barmharttigheid

God's name is mercy

El nombre de Dios: Misericordia

Il nome di Dio: è la Misericordia

Gottes Name: Barmherzigkeit

하느님의 이름은 자비로움이다

De naam van God is:
barmhartigheid

+ [illegible] + [illegible]

Aphorism 54

La plus belle musique est parfois le silence

Stilte is de mooiste muziek

The most beautiful music is sometimes silence

La más bella música es algunas veces el silencio

Il silenzio è la musica più bella

Manchmal ist Stille die schönste Musik

가장 아름다운 음악은 때로는 침묵이다

Stilte is de mooiste muziek

Pour être heureux il faut prendre le temps

Gelukkig worden vraagt tijd

To be happy takes time

Para ser feliz hay que tomar su tiempo

Per essere felici, occorre del tempo

Glücklich werden braucht Zeit

행복하기 위해서는 시간이 필요하다

Gelukkig worden
vraagt tijd

Aphorism 56

La pluie ne crave le soleil

Regen doet hunkeren naar de zon

Rain does make you hanker for the sun

La lluvia hace desear el sol

La pioggia fa di hanker per il sole

Im Regen streben wir nach der Sonne

비는 우리에게 태양을 갈망하게 한다

Regen doet verlangen
naar de zon
+ Godfried Kard. Danneels

Plus que donner, Dieu par-donne

Er is geven, maar er is meer: ver-geven

More than giving, God for-gives.

Más que dar, Dios per-dona

Più che donare, Dio per-dona

Mehr als geben: Gott ver-gibt

주는 것보다 더 귀한 것은 하느님께서 용서해 주시는 것이다

Er is geven
Maar er is meer:
ver-geven

Dieu donne: il ne demande que peu

God vraagt niet veel, maar Hij geeft alles

God gives: he asks for very little

Dios da mucho y pide poco

Dio dona: non domanda che poca cosa

Gott fordert wenig, geben tut er alles

하느님은 주실 뿐 요구하지 않으신다

God vraagt niet veel.
Maar Hij geeft alles

Aphorism 59

Dire 'bon-jour' donne la joie au vision

'Goeie dag' zeggen maakt de buur blij

To say 'good-day' gives joy to one's neighbour

Decir 'buenos días' da alegría al vecino

Dire 'buongiorno' dona gioia al vicino

'Guten Tag' sagen, macht den Nachbarn froh

<인사>는 이웃에게 기쁨을 전하는 것이다

zeggen 'goeie dag'
maakt de boeren
blij

Aphorism 60

Qui se regarde ne juge pas autrui

Wie zichzelf bekijkt oordeeelt niemand anders

Those who look at themselves do not judge others

Quién se mira así mismo no juzga a los demás

Colui che guarda a se stesso non giudica gli altri

Wer sich selbst anschaut, urteilt nicht über andere

자신을 돌아보는 사람은 다른 이를 판단하지 않는다

Wie zichzelf bekijkt
oordeelt niemand
anders

CPSIA information can be obtained
at www.ICGtesting.com
Printed in the USA
LVXC01n0829251017
553513LV00002B/13
* 9 7 8 1 9 2 5 4 3 8 1 6 1 *